PLYMOUTH
THROUGH THE LENS

VOLUME TWO

COMPILED BY
BRIAN MOSELEY

B. S. MOSELEY
PLYMOUTH   DEVON
1985

ISBN 0 901676 07 1
First published: December 1985
Text © Brian Moseley 1985

British Library Cataloguing in Publication Data:

Plymouth: through the lens.
Vol. 2
1. Plymouth (Devon) — History — Pictorial works
I. Moseley, Brian
942.3'580855'0222

ISBN   0-90167607—1   DA690.P7

Published by B. S. Moseley, 21 Pennycross Park Road, Plymouth, and printed by Hitchings and Mason Ltd., West Hoe Road, Plymouth, Devon.

LIST OF ILLUSTRATIONS

ACKNOWLEDGEMENTS

I should like to record my thanks to the following people for their assistance in the preparation of this volume:

Mr. T. Besterman, Curator, and Mr. W. H. Scutt, Assistant Keeper of Archaeology & Local History, Plymouth City Museum and Art Gallery;

Mr. Brandon Coombes, Central Reprographic Services, Civic Centre;

Mr. R. E. Jess of Hitchings & Mason Ltd.;

The Western Morning News Co. Ltd.;

Mrs. M. Jewell;

Mr. Gilbert Corran;

and Mrs. A. R. Skinner, Mrs. E. Lamb and Mr. J. Smith of the Plymouth Local History Library, for their patience and good humour in trying to find answers to my questions while dealing with a dozen other things at the same time.

Brian Moseley

Over the centuries, as Plymouth has grown, many of the old Lanes have become Roads and some have vanished forever. Where, for instance, was Gooseberry Lane? Surprisingly it still exists although it no longer carries its name. The picture above shows it in October 1952.

Gooseberry Lane ran from Millbay Road up to Citadel Road and Mount Pleasant. King Street Methodist Church and the DHSS offices now stand on either corner.

Colonial House, bearing the date 1919, housed Coast Lines Ltd, the shipping agents, and the Plymouth branch of the Royal National Lifeboat Institution. Coast Lines later became part of Travellers Ltd. local agents for the Royal Mail Line. In the 1950s they were also agents for Amarda Self-Drive cars, chiefly Ford Anglias, Prefects and Consuls.

At the rear of the building is James Dowling's Westminster Garage, originally part of the Westminster Hotel which was bombed. In April 1949 Travellers Ltd. were going to repair these premises but the City decided it wanted the site for redevelopment. In March 1952 Colonial House was purchased for £5,500 and it was demolished early in 1954 at a cost of £180.

(City Museum)

This picture of Heath's Hotel, at 39 George Street, was taken in May 1950.

At the beginning of the last century these premises were occupied by Murch & Company. By the 1930s it was Cousin's Family Hotel, owned by Sam Roseman. At that time Genoni's Swiss Restaurant was next door and nearby was Limpenny's Umbrella Shop (later Bonney's Restaurant) and the office of R. Hansford Worth, the civil engineer.

An advert placed in the *Western Evening Herald* in February 1945 announced that Cousin's Hotel would henceforth be known as the "Bodega" and that it would be 'exclusively for Men'.

In July 1949 the Council bought the premises for £45,000, including the licence, fixtures and fittings, and loose chattels. It was then re-let to Starkey, Knight and Ford for a period of five years, later extended, at £1,800 per annum. It finally closed early in November 1958 when the lease expired.

Around that time a bottle of Gordon's Gin cost £1 5s 3d while a pint of draught Bass Pale Ale would have been about 1/8d. A small Guinness cost 1/2d and a large Stout was about 1/5d.

(City Museum)

This picture taken in September 1949 shows Raleigh Street as seen from the side of the Regent/Odeon Cinema. Frankfort Street runs left to right. The old Plymouth Co-operative building stood on the corner where the men are seen digging.

Phillips & Bray, the corn merchants, originally occupied South Devon House. Fruit and vegetable merchants A. H. Smale & Sons moved in sometime in the mid-1930s. The garage type premises was Josiah Williams' coach works while the tall rather ornate building was the Plymouth Brethren Gospel Hall.

Note the Gaumont Cinema advert strategically placed right opposite the Odeon!

(City Museum)

The parish of All Saints, Harwell Street, was created in 1875 and work started immediately on erecting a church. Owing to lack of funds the building was not completed by the time the Reverend Charles Chase was appointed vicar in 1877. A Londoner, the Reverend Chase had entered the Army at the age of 16 and when he left eight years later was a lieutenant in the 21st Hussars. He was ordained in 1871.

On arriving at All Saints and finding his church still incomplete, he set about raising funds. In the end he not only managed to complete the church (in 1910) but also bought No. 5 Henry Street as a Mission Hall and Numbers 6 to 9 to house the All Saints' Institute for Working Men.

For a few years immediately after the blitz it was used as a store by A. C. Stidwill Ltd, the fruit and potato merchants, but by the time of this photo, November 1953, it was empty and ready for demolition.

(City Museum)

This photograph of Numbers 3 to 8 Cambridge Street was taken in January 1955.

John Richards, at No. 3, not only sold cooked meats and other groceries but also sold pasties and sandwiches. Louisa and George Warn ran the greengrocers next to the Empire Inn.

The imposing structure in between the two shops was in 1897 the residence of Mr. J. B. Foster, architect, at No. 4, and Miss E. R. Foster at No. 5 on the right. Possibly he designed the premises himself.

(City Museum)

A closer view of the Empire Inn, Cambridge Street, is provided by this picture, also taken in January 1955. George Dunbar was licencee here before the War and Mr. M. L. Hockaday in the 1950s.

Spence's newsagency stood on the corner of Cambridge Lane West. Before the War it had been William Thomas' fruit shop.

In 1958 the *Western Evening Herald* cost "Twopence Half-penny". *Titbits* was 4d and a copy of *Woman's Own* cost 5d. Teenagers could get the *Roxy* for 4d and have a free Pete Murray 6.05 Special song book! A Mars bar cost about 3½d.

(City Museum)

Numbers 13, 14 & 15 Cambridge Street are shown in this photograph from 1955.

"Helena" was the property of a Mrs. Mackenny. She specialised in Sally Slade and Linda Leigh designs. Before the War the shop was occupied by Harold Elford the hairdresser.

Number 15 had been a dairy for over half a century, the last owner being Harry Radmore. It is seen here as Mrs. Dulling's general store where she no doubt sold sugar at 2½d per lb, tea at about 1/10½d a quarter, and butter at 2/- a lb.

A ladies coat would have cost around ten guineas which was just about a weeks wages for a skilled man. However, with income tax at nine shillings in the pound, he would have had to save hard! There were also two types of bikini on sale, one for 19/11d and an "extra brief" for 12/11d.

Cornwall Street now slices through this block of buildings.

(City Museum)

Opposite Mrs. Dulling's shop in Cambridge Street was the Cambridge Arms. It backed on to the Odeon Cinema.

James Lewis and George Popham both held the licence prior to the blitz.

Tivvy Home Brew cost 8½d a half-pint when the Cambridge closed its doors on August 8th 1954. This photograph was taken the following day and within twelve months this had become Cornwall Street.

(City Museum)

Cambridge Lane West from the King Street end of King Gardens towards Oxford Street. Cambridge Street is to the right of the picture. It was really only a back lane but it did have some addresses of its own and this photo shows Numbers 30 to 36, the latter being nearest the camera.

Back at the beginning of the century, these houses were occupied by a moulder, a tailor, a shoemaker, a plumber and a foreman of the Great Western Railway.

At the top end of the Lane was the mineral water factory of J. H. Furguson & Sons. James Henry himself used to live at 38 King Gardens. By 1960 the company was being run by Mr. P. Waldron.

In the 1930s Fred Davies had his upholstery works in the Lane.

The brick wall on the right is on the corner of a lane which led out to Spence's newsagency in Cambridge Street (see page 10).

(City Museum)

Tracy Street Ope linked King Gardens to the left with Tracy Street. It was formerly known as Morley Street West. The white building on the extreme right was Tracy Cottage.

The house bearing the nameplate was actually known as 35a King Gardens. The double-fronted one next to it was 35b. At Number 35 itself — just out of view — the Tucker family ran a drapery business.

Before the War, Thomas Leaman combined building with undertaking at the premises seen here occupied by Stanley Griffin. The shop on the opposite corner of Tracy Street was run by Mrs. M. Stanbury, who succeeded Mrs. Northcott.

On the north side of the Ope was the printing works of W. J. Jacobs; by 1951 it was George Smale's fruit warehouse. This photo is dated January 1955.

(City Museum)

The south side of Morley Street Ope presents a sorry sight in this picture from January 1955. It was another four years before the area was placed under a compulsory purchase order.

On the corner of Cambridge Street (to the left) was a fish and chip shop which at this time belonged to a Mr. Redvers Parsons. To the right of the picture was Cambridge Lane West.

Numbers 1, 2 and 3 the Ope are obviously empty but in the early 1930s they housed five businesses. A. E. Welchman, tailor, and J. Lintern, bootmaker, occupied Number One. Next door was shared by H. Hardaker, cleaners and dyers, and R. T. England, garage. Where on earth did he keep the cars? Number Three was where Blanche Perring dispensed sweets and chocolates.

(City Museum)

15

The view up Russell Street from Frankfort Street was somewhat dominated by the Co-op Wholesale Society's warehouse on the corner of York Street and Morley Street.

D. & E. Shoe Repairs Ltd. moved from Number 27 Russell Street to Westwell Street in 1954 when this area was about to be demolished to make way for Cornwall Street. They had branches in Exeter, Newton Abbot and Bideford and their familiar advertisement on the side of the Corporation buses read "Fair Wear or a Free Repair".

When the Tudor Restaurant moved up to Ebrington Street at the end of 1952, Number 26 was taken over by Dingle's carpet department. At No. 25 was pork butcher Ernest Stephens, whose father had the shop way back at the end of the last century. Shortly after this picture was taken, in February 1952, they moved to Number 18, next door to Russells the grocers.

Note the shops on the left which appear in the next picture.

(City Museum)

16

A demolition discount of 4/- in the £ was being offered by Wray & Co., and B. R. Burge Ltd. when this photograph was taken in June 1954.

Wray, Bertie Burge and the Checkers Cafe all occupied what was No. 17 Russell Street, a very notable address. This was the home of Hoyten & Coles, the printers, who in 1899 had acquired the copyright of Doidge's Western Counties Illustrated Annual. They continued to publish it at this address for some 40 years before they removed to Whimple Street in the early 1930s.

Coster's Thrift and Savings office was at No. 1 Morley Street. It was here that Florrie Vosper started her wireless supplies business in the 1930s. When she moved further up Russell Street (see page 19), Frank Vosper turned the shop over to bicycles. She also used part of Number 17 as a general shop for a while just prior to the outbreak of War, while Horace Colwill used another part as a ladies hairdresser.

The Checkers Cafe belonged to A. L. Williams and fish and grills were served from 10.30 a.m. till 2 p.m. and from 3 till 6 p.m.

(City Museum)

Next door to Wray's was the Russell Arms resplendent in the familiar black and white decor of the Starkey, Knight and Ford brewery empire. Their Black Horse bottled beer was advertised as "The bottle beer with a kick in it".

Tivvy Brown and Tivvy Special cost 1/3d a pint while a pint of draught Bass was 1/8d. George Moffatt was licencee for part of the 1930s.

The lane down the side of the pub was Willow Plot. The photograph is dated June 1954.

(City Museum)

Now you see it — now you don't! Within a month of the last picture, the Russell Arms has been reduced to a pile of rubble. This is now looking west along Cornwall Street!

In the early 1930s Mrs. Florence Vosper started a wireless shop at No. 1 Morley Street (see page 17). By 1935 it was in the name of Doris Vosper and a second shop had been opened here at No. 15 Russell Street, in what had been Fred Warne's fruit shop. By the outbreak of War, it had become Vospers Radio (Plymouth) Ltd.

A radio licence cost £1 until August 1965 when it was increased to £1 5s.

Vospers stocked radio sets from Bush, Ekco, Kolster-Brandes, Phillips, Philco, Pye, Ultra, Furguson, Ferranti, Marconi and McMichael.

Number 14 housed William Willis, the butcher. He sold Fresh Sausages, Hog Puddings, Pickled Hams and Tongues, and claimed "Nothing but English Meat Sold". He also sold Pure Beef Dripping and Lard, both here and at his other shop at 2 West Street, Tavistock. In this photograph, dated July 1954, his old shop carries the names of Dick Kell Flooring and the Universal Book Store.

(City Museum)

19

The rear of Woolworth's is just visible in this view of 12, 12A and 13 Russell Street.

Willow Street led past Arch Lane and St. Andrew's Mission Chapel to Frankfort Street.

Before the War, No. 12 was occupied by confectioner Mrs. Emily Marsh, while 12A — here Goodbody's — was L. C. and R. R. Steed's XL Dairy. Perhaps they sold Devon Cream which at the time of this picture, July 1954, was 3s for a quarter pound sent by post. They had taken over this business from Fred Palmer and also had shops at Saltash Street, Hender's Corner and Crownhill.

Fred Elworthy's wool shop was situated next door at Number 13. It was later taken over by the Aberdeen Wool Company.

Note the taping on the windows. This was to help prevent the glass from flying when it was shattered by bomb blasts.

(City Museum)

This picture from December 1953 shows the Welcome Inn, at 9 Richmond Street. Harold Stewart brewed his own beer here before the War. James Redding was licencee before that.

Next door, where the cars are parked, Minnie Hutchings sold second-hand furniture while the building next to it, just visible, was the Millbay Laundry garage and receiving office. Until 1923 this had been the premises of the Central Steam Laundry and back at the end of last century was the Richmond Brewery.

(City Museum)

An old "Slow — Major Road Ahead" sign adds a bit of interest to this November 1953 view down Richmond Street. Numbers 2 and 3 Morley Street can be seen at the bottom, beyond the coach.

The house nearest the camera is No. 51. Perry and Campbell's tyre shop had previously been the home of plumber Alfred Maunder. Number 53 had at one time been a beer house.

Regretfully the coach has not been identified.

(City Museum)

Probably the only reason the streets were clear of parked cars in the 1950s was that there were plenty of bomb sites to act as car parks, as is shown in this picture of Richmond Street at its junction with York Street.

The photo shows Numbers 55 to 59 as they were in November 1953, just prior to demolition.

Wilfred Bayley had been the hairdresser at No. 56 and Frank Harris sold all manner of musical instruments next door. George Mead sold furniture at The White Shop until Harding & Sons took over after being bombed out of 161-163 Union Street. The end shop was where Fred Ralph sold tripe. The remaining shops in the row are pictured on page 26 of *Vanishing Plymouth*.

Immediately after the War a utility bedroom suite cost around £90 but by the early 1950s the price had come down to around £65. An oak lounge suite would have cost around £48. A baby grand piano could have set you back £157 whilst an E-flat alto saxophone could have been yours for £16. The cost of tripe went unrecorded.

(City Museum)

This excellent picture of Pennycomequick was taken in 1949. On the right, behind the RAF recruiting poster, is the ruins of what was once Joel and Clare Roberts' nursery. Although the glass-houses remained, Joel moved to Windsor Terrace to live and Miss Olwen Davey used the premises as a confectionery for a couple of years. It was disused by 1938 and the land was used by local lads as a cycle racing track.

The tram tracks from Plymouth to Milehouse and Paradise Road are clearly visible, as are the old tram poles, especially the striped one in the middle of the junction. The Plymouth trams from West Hoe and the Devonport ones from Fore Street both terminated here until October 1916 when a connection was laid in following the amalgamation of the Three Towns. The line up Alma Road to Milehouse was added in 1922 and was soon being served by the 9, 10 and 14 routes.

Note the policeman quietly surveying the scene and, on the left, the police telephone post and the triangular bus stop.

(City Museum)

By March 1953 Pennycomequick had been transformed. Yet what a happy scene of care-free motoring this picture presents.

Mr. and Mrs. L. H. Cook were doubtless getting ready to serve "English and Continental Snacks" to their lunchtime regulars at the Pennycomequick in competition with Long & Enon's chip shop directly across the roundabout, near the Evans Stove Works store.

John Francis looked after the little post office and the sign over the warehouse used by OXO Ltd. was a familiar sight from the top deck of buses gliding down Alma Road.

The buses had been given their own bus-bay down by the old police pillar box. The service 19 to Ford called here about 6½ minutes after leaving its terminus on Royal Parade.

Note the Plymouth and Devonport boundary stones at bottom right. The boundary line ran across Saltash Road to the corner of the OXO warehouse and the Stove Works. Thus the lady standing at the bus stop was in Plymouth while the other stop, behind the lamp, was really in Devonport!

(City Museum)

Above: "Build your own TV set for under £16" proclaims the advert outside Maine Books at Number 8 North Hill Terrace.

C. Mayne & Co. Ltd. was one of 13 booksellers in Plymouth in 1955. No doubt they were stocking copies of R. A. J. Walling's *Story of Plymouth* at 15s, almost the only local history book available at that time. What an easy time the booksellers had then: only 18,188 titles were issued in 1954 compared with over 50,000 in 1984. Mayne Books survived only until January 1957 when it went into liquidation.

The photograph is dated February 1954.

(City Museum)

Opposite: What a great pity this stylish building did not survive the post-war redevelopment. Note especially the embellishments on the far end of the building and the lion head tops to the rain water pipes.

Picken & Company, wine and spirit merchants, was founded at 24 Whimple Street in 1857 by Messrs Picken and Curgenven. By 1949 it was owned by Popplestones and sold Bass, William Youngers', Truman's, Tiverton Beer and Guinness "Harp Label" Stout. Note the "Bar for Gentlemen" sign.

Scaffolding surrounds the Royal Insurance building which was nearing completion when this picture was taken in July 1954.

(City Museum)

In May 1950 the five shops which made up Friary Gate were reported to be in a dangerous condition. When the photographer passed by in December 1950 only Number 1, Jordan's newsagency, was still in business. By the following July the row had been demolished at a cost of just £72 4s.

Friary Gate was situated in Exeter Street, between Fred Smith's tobacconists shop at the entrance to Friary Goods Yard and Salem Street.

Next to Jordan's was boot repairer William Yates and at Number 3 Jean Abbott sold bedroom furniture before it became a drug store. At Number 4 was the County's only bird cage maker, Ronald Nixon. He also sold seed and pet foods. The end shop was a hairdressers.

(City Museum)

Further up Exeter Street from Friary Gate, opposite Brunswick Terrace, was Dustan's general store. It was the property of Janie Pearse in the pre-war years.

Prices are always interesting. In 1958 when this photograph was taken Pan Yan Pickel was "on offer" for 1/7d, a saving of 3d a jar. At the same time Typhoo Tea was selling at 1/9d a quarter, apples were about 1/3d a pound and cheese cost around 2/6d to 3s per lb. Golden Shred marmalade was around 1/5d and Dustan's no doubt stocked the ½lb and 1lb tins of Lyles Golden Syrup.

Bennett's saffron flour could be purchased in one pound packets for 1/- and Stork Margarine came in ½lb blocks for 10½d. Crispbread was available then; Dar-Vita cost 11d for a ½lb packet. Crawford's wholemeal chocolate biscuits were 1/5½d a packet while a large bottle of Jafferade cost 10d. Park Drive cigarettes were 1/3d for ten.

(City Museum)

Manor Street lay on the boundary between Plymouth and Stonehouse, the line running along the wall on the left of this picture. This building was used as a biscuit store and then in the 1950s by Smiths Potato Crisps Ltd.

Of the premises on the right (i.e. in Plymouth), the one nearest the camera was Henry Rockey's snack bar. This was on the corner of Rendle Street. Three doors away was R. E. Hannam the coal dealer. This business had been started last century by James Diver. It later passed to Ernest Penney. At the time of this photo (February 1954) coal was over £7 10s a ton, a price which soon doubled.

Mrs. S. Wellington attended to gents hair at Number 3 while a couple of doors away — across Alice Street — was Mrs. Hoskin's grocery, in what had been Ernie Fletcher's outfitting store.

The last blacksmith in Stonehouse had his forge in Manor Street. In 1956 Fred Bassett could still be seen shoeing horses, carrying on a craft brought to the Street some 60 years earlier by John Mallett.

(City Museum)

In April 1954 the Duke of Cornwall Public House stood on its own at Number 66 High Street, Stonehouse. This was on the south side, near the corner of Market Street and directly opposite Waterloo Street.

At the beginning of the century it was Number 71 and W. J. Jago was the landlord. Since then George Harris, George Lilly and Ernest Tottel have pulled pints here, the last being Howard Newnham who also held the licenses of the Chimes Tavern, the Criterion, the Fellowship, the Jamaica House, the Queen & Constitution, the Regent, the United Services Inn, and the Warn Hotel in Anstis Street.

Just a few doors away Jessie May Burrows had run a small general shop.

Plymouth Brewery's beer cost 1/1d a pint while bitter and mild were 1/6d. Cider was cheaper at only 9d a pint.

(City Museum)

The Talbot Hotel is the only building now left standing which will help to locate this July 1953 view of Union Street, Stonehouse. St. Mary Street cuts across the foreground.

Underwoods was an old established grocery store which at one time was also a receiving office for the Great Western Railway. They also used the Lamson Paragon cash/change wire system similar to the old Woolworths at Devonport.

Next door at Number 13 was the Stonehouse Branch Post Office. At the end of last century, first class post meant that a letter posted here at 8 p.m. would be delivered in Plymouth later that same evening.

Then came Wilson Brothers' shell fish shop, established in 1905. They stayed open until 11 p.m. and not only sold crab and lobster sandwiches but would send crabs by post to any address. Beyond them was the Prince Arthur Public House and, in the gap, the Ebeneezer Baptist Chapel.

Across the other side of the Street were Pooley's the bakers, Edgar Thorne (hairdresser), Pankhurst of Weymouth (motor cycles), Bennett's pet food store and then the West India House Hotel.

(City Museum)

The bunting is out, the flags are flying and all is well with the world for this picture was taken just two days after the Coronation celebrations of June 1953. That evening the Plymouth Choral Society presented "Merrie England" in the Hoe Marquee. Tickets cost half a crown.

Standing grandly at the corner of Edgcumbe Street and Brownlow Street is the Methodist Church which was erected in 1813, just two years before Union Street was built across the marshland.

At Number 1 Union Street was Vosper's tobacconists shop. The Union Jack is flying over the door of Mrs. Winifred Pullein's drapery store. An empty space and a dustbin mark the site of the old Stonehouse Social Club, previously the home of the Liberal Club.

Howard Newnham followed James Maunder as the licencee of the Criterion Inn. The empty fish cart stands where once was Phillips Tattoo Saloon.

Dot Bell's cafe displays a Coronation poster. Open all night, she also offered Bed and Board for 35s a week. Ernest Buckley's Cycle Depot was here before he moved along to Number 11.

(City Museum)

33

It was in 1898 that Harold Roberts had erected a fine purpose-built building to house his cleaning and dyeing business. Architect Mr. H. J. Snell designed the limestone and brick structure which was situated at Victoria Place, Stonehouse, next to the Battery Hill Quarry. It was but a short walk from the shop in Millbay Road, Plymouth, where it had all started.

This photograph, taken in December 1953, shows what was left of the original works of the Millbay Laundry, Cleaning & Dyeing Co. Ltd. after the bombing of April 21st, 1941. Harry Roberts died in the August no doubt heartbroken at the damage done to his fine headquarters. The nearby Eddystone works remained almost intact.

The building was only two storeys high. The doorway nearest the camera led into the reception area and where the wall has completely gone was a group of three arched windows which were shaded by a sun blind.

It is interesting to note that the cost of having a suit cleaned in the 1930s was 3/6d, the same as it was in 1897!

(City Museum)

On August 1st, 1951 the Duke of Edinburgh paid his first visit to Plymouth. He presented new King's Colours and Regimental Colours to the Royal Marines at Stonehouse Barracks.

Earlier that year, in January in fact, this was the scene at the north-western end of the Barracks, where Barrack Place joined Durnford Street.

There were six properties, Number 1 being the Royal Standard Public House which stood on the corner with Emma Place. The other five, including numbers 5 and 6 pictured here, were all houses although Number 5 had at one time been a beer house. At No. 6 once lived a sergeant of the Royal Marine Light Infantry.

The end building, partly slate hung, was Number 1 Durnford Street, for over twenty-five years the home of John Tabb.

Barrack Place was apparently going to be used for an extension of Stonehouse Barracks but the authorities changed their minds and in July 1946 the area was released for demolition and redevelopment.

(City Museum)

If our intrepid photographer, the late Leslie Fenn, had not had the foresight to take this picture in November 1950, it is doubtful whether these structures would have ever been recorded.

It was in January 1945 that the Corporation first authorised the erection of temporary bungalows to alleviate the post-war housing shortage. By November 1946, one thousand had been put up and eventually a total of 2,314 prefabs existed in the City.

The seventeen erected at King's Road, Devonport, were of the American two bedroom type and included a gas or electric cooker and a refrigerator. They were given odd numbers between 1 and 33 and had a fairly pleasant outlook over Stonehouse Lake.

At the beginning of 1960 it was decided to remove these prefabs which were on sites designated as "open spaces" and by October these had gone together with others at Parkside, Keyham. It was to be another twelve years before all the City's "temporary bungalows" had vanished.

(City Museum)

It is not clear exactly why this one house in eighteenth century George Street, Devonport, should look so much grander that its neighbours but it may have something to do with the fact that in 1850 it was the residence of a Captain Robert Ross. Presumably he was a military officer rather than a naval one as by the end of the century Number 6 had become Staff Sergeants' Quarters. Even as late as 1932 it was Soldiers' Married Quarters so perhaps the property was owned by the military authorities.

At Number 10 lived the Reverend George Proctor MA, the vicar of St. Stephens (see *Plymouth Through the Lens No. 1*).

The photograph is dated December 1955.

(City Museum)

This was the state of Colin Richard's old shop in George Street, Devonport, in September 1953.

Like so many other premises in Devonport, Number 57, on the corner with Pembroke Street, had been a beer house. Mr. Richards made it into a general store circa 1934.

The shop on the right was a grocers for a long time but just before the War Arthur Mitchell ran it as a newsagents. At the time of the photo it was a hairdressers.

Note Mary Bassett's shop in Pembroke Street, by the road sign. In the distance is the Himalaya Inn.

By 1955 the only building left on the north side of Pembroke Street was Number 56, behind the camerman, which had previously been the Musketry Arms.

(City Museum)

For drinking establishments it was difficult to beat Pembroke Street, Devonport.

In 1899 there were: the Royal Exchange; the George Inn; the Royal Sovereign; the Albion Inn (pictured in *Vanishing Plymouth*); the Jolly Bacchus; the Bristol Vaults; the Musketry Arms; the Rose & Crown; the Himalaya Inn; not to mention the Half Moon and the King's Arms which still survive today. And there were seven beer houses!

The Himalaya was on the north side and this photograph was taken looking up Stanley Street towards Mount Street. It was taken in June 1954. While Robert Clabon pulled the pints, next door at Number 36 William Marshall would be dishing out fish and chips.

Before 1885 the pub was known as the Cornish Arms; it was recorded as such in 1850.

(City Museum)

Perhaps the most interesting revelation of this photograph is the way it shows how these houses in Pembroke Street were constructed. They dated from about 1780 when this was known as Liberty Street.

The three-wheeled milk cart belonged to Sidney Downing. He ran the dairy at Number 43, just out of view, which had previously belonged to Charles Farley. Leo Bustin was the hairdresser at Number 46 (see the following picture) while a Miss Phillips looked after the fish and chip shop next door. This had previously been in the hands of Mrs. Bessie Banbury. On the far right is George Wilkinson's greengrocery shop.

February 1951 was when the photograph was taken.

(City Museum)

These two properties were Numbers 62 and 63 Pembroke Street and were photographed in October 1954. The lane is St. Stephen's Street which led through to Clowance Street.

The end shop was in the hands of the Smith family during the 1930s but just prior to the War, Mrs. Kathleen Lakeman was using it as a wardrobe store.

During the thirties Bustin's Hair Saloon was situated at Number 63 but by 1939 Frank Skinner was using the premises as a post office and stationers.

(City Museum)

This block of buildings stood opposite the Himalaya Inn in Pembroke Street. The van is parked at the corner of Stanley Street.

Note how Number 76 was much taller than the rest of the block. This housed newsagent George White. At Number 78 was Emily Smith's dairy. The shops at 80 and 81 were occupied by George Pitcher the butcher and greengrocer Fred Clarke.

Pembroke Street was quite a self-contained little community before the War. It had no fewer than ten general shops and five butchers including a branch of Eastmans. Most other trades were represented. There were four hairdressers, four furniture shops, three fish and chip shops, three boot repairers, two dairies plus a newsagent, tailor, draper, coal merchant, baker, printer, post office and stationer, greengrocer and a tobacconist. There was hardly any need to go to the shops in Fore Street!

This photograph was taken in October 1954.

(City Museum)

Numbers 47 to 53 James Street, Devonport, had already been empty for about three years when this photograph was taken one sunny Tuesday in June 1954.

Just out of view to the left is the Dockyard wall. The car is passing the junction with Edinburgh Road, to the left, and Mount Street.

The premises on the corner with Pembroke Street was originally the Royal Exchange Public House. It later became a confectioners and by the outbreak of War was Mrs. Florence Evan's general store. Although a Mrs. Thomas had the shop in the early 1950s, the houses in James Street were already empty and there was not much left of Pembroke Street, so business must have been pretty quiet. By 1953 it was boarded up.

(City Museum)

Opposite: Like the earlier picture of George Street, this view of Number 30 Duke Street, Devonport, is chiefly of interest for the way it shows the construction of the house. What a dark place it must have been with only one window on the first floor.

Duke Street dated from the 1750s and Number 30 was right opposite St. John's Church, between Duke Street Ope and Ker Street Ope. Nurse Mary Hunter lived here in the 1930s.

At Number 32 Mr. J. Curtis and later Mrs. Parry sold groceries, sweets, stationery and fancy goods.

The photo is dated May 1955. *(City Museum)*

This picture from November 1954 shows Numbers 14 and 15 Cumberland Street, Devonport. Number 15 had always been a chemists. A Mr. Perkins ran it for a long time until in the early 1930s it was taken over by Prout & West Ltd. A J. Bolt acquired the shop in the 1940s when part of the building was also used by the General Supplies Club, a furnishing club.

K. C. Slee & Son, the butchers, occupied what had been Stanbury's gown shop.

(City Museum)

Opposite: This picture from September 1953 shows the north side of Duke Street, near to its junction with Catherine Street.

The first building is Number 5. James Patten, the market superintendent, lived over the market gateway. Charles Bond ran a general store at No. 7 before the War. George Marsden's Devon Cafe is also visible.

On the right of the photo can be seen the barber's pole of Fred Burrows' hairdressing shop. On the corner was Mr. Davey's shop, previously Brimacombe's cooked meat shop.

(City Museum)

Above: The Salvation Army Naval and Military Hostel first appeared in Catherine Street, Devonport, in 1898 when they took over the premises of plumber J. R. Gill at Number 12. Number 11 was acquired around 1913 and then a few years later Jones' Refreshment House at Number 8 became the Naval & Military Meeting House.

This left toy dealers Bennett & Son in the middle at Numbers 9 and 10 but by 1928 these too had been added to the Hostel which then stretched from Numbers 8 to 12.

(City Museum)

Opposite: King Street, Devonport, ran between Granby Street and Cannon Street and dated from around 1730.

This photograph from April 1951 shows Number 32 which throughout the 1930s was Griffith's furniture store. The shop backed on to the Devonport Assembly Rooms in Morice Street.

Another business in King Street was "Ye Olde Curiousity Shop" which was actually a general store run by James Conway.

The Lord Hood Public House stood on the corner with Cannon Street.

(City Museum)

Above: Back lanes are not normally very important and few of them actually have names. This picture, taken in February 1954, is of Jessamine Lane, Devonport, which ran parallel with King and Queen Streets from Albany Street northwards to Cannon Street.

Next to the house was the back entrance to the old Eagle Brewery, which from about 1923 was used as a bottling plant by Saccone & Speed.

Other businesses in the Lane were furniture dealer Alfred Furze, cycle repairer Albert Collings and timber merchant John Bowden. In 1954 only the Western Counties Builders & Decorators Ltd. remained. *(City Museum)*

Opposite the Salvation Army Hall in Granby Street, Devonport, stood the general store and dairy belonging to Mrs. Alice Elizabeth Doolin.

She had taken over from her husband Philip. He had taken over the shop around 1930 from a Mr. Knight, who may have been Alice's father as he lived with them for many years afterwards. It is thought that the shop never re-opened after suffering bomb damage.

The photograph is dated May 1952.

(City Museum)

It was around 1903 that Ayers & Sons first moved into Number 12 Granby Street, Devonport. The shop on the ground floor was then known as the Empire Stores. It was not long before Ayers took over that floor as well and remained there for over fifty years. Their telephone number was Devonport 148.

On the other side of Granby Street Ope is the general store and dairy run by Mrs. Alice Doolin. The shop was almost opposite the Salvation Army Hall pictured in *Volume One*.

The roof of a building in the New Granby Barracks can be seen in the background of this picture taken in March 1955.

(City Museum)

It was in 1893 that Mr. J. W. B. Swainson took over the chemists shop at 22 Albert Road which had been run by a Mr. R. S. Coke.

William Barrett appeared on the scene in 1906 and within six years the business had moved next door to Number 21, the premises illustrated here. At this time he was also listed as a dentist.

Mr. Swainson is not mentioned again until 1935 when the business was known as Barrett & Swainson. William Barrett lived over the shop.

This photograph was taken in November 1959. Charlotte Street is visible in the background. Note the temporary premises housing the Albert Fisheries. The cheapest fish at that time was Whiting at 1/2d a lb. Kippers were between 1/2d and 1/8d and cod fillets 1/10d to 2/3d per lb. Haddock could be as much as 2/9d per lb.

Remember those 3½d strips of Aspro? No doubt the chemists also stocked SR Toothpaste (1/4d) and Germolene sunburn cream at 1/4d or 3/3d including purchase tax.

(City Museum)

Not much can be said about Number 106 Albert Road, Devonport. This block was situated between Ross Street and Garden Street, almost opposite the Friendship Inn. This picture, taken in May 1952, has been included as a record of the houses which existed on the site now occupied by Aggie Weston's.

Note how the railings managed to escape being "called up" for war service. Presumably this was because their removal would have created a danger as there would then be nothing to prevent someone falling down into the basement.

The "Drink Vimto" sign in the window of the Albert Fisheries fish and chip shop will be familiar to readers. Vim Tonic, to give it its full name, was first made in Salford, Manchester, in 1908 by John Nichols. During the 1950s it was widely available in chip shops and snack bars at 3d or 4d for a 6oz bottle. It was bottled locally by Bracher & Sturgess of Southside Street. Vimto is now enjoying renewed popularity.

(City Museum)

Dockyard Halt on the Great Western Railway between Devonport and Keyham opened 80 years ago, on June 1st 1905. But it was not until 1928 that Mr. L. J. Beale opened his little general store at Number 1 Cross Hill, Stoke. Previous to that there were only the two houses of Cross Hill Villas in this vicinity.

Six years after it opened, the shop was sold to Rupert Ghillyer and then to Fred Jago. The premises survived the nearby bombing of April 21st 1941 and were photographed in July 1950. A few years later the business was in the name of Adams & Mosley.

Surprisingly, the three garages shown in this picture were officially Numbers 2, 3 & 4 Cross Hill! At Number 5 was a hairdresser, next to that was Arthur Robinson's fish and chip shop, and then a drapers.

It is unfortunately no longer possible to drive under the railway to St. Vincent Street. Note the old "Low Bridge" sign.

(City Museum)

St. Peter's Chapel at Saltash Passage was actually in the County of Cornwall when it was opened in 1886. The Passage belonged to the Honour of Trematon and thus was part of Cornwall until the boundary was revised in 1895.

Built as a Mission Chapel on land given by Lady Compton, St. Peter's was dedicated to the memory of Admiral Sir Peter Richards KCB. In 1826 he was Commander of the Sloop *Pelorus* and in September 1828 he was promoted to Captain. Later, as a Rear Admiral, he was Flag Officer at Greenwich Hospital and for a short while he was a Lord Commissioner of the Admiralty. He died early in 1869.

The Chapel was situated between Little Ash Gardens and Little Ash Road. It was damaged during the raids of April 1941. It was photographed in February 1954.

(City Museum)

This charming rural scene is sadly no longer rural and certainly not charming. The cottage has gone, so have some of the trees, the road is much wider and it is definitely much busier. In short, Honicknowle Lane looks nothing like this today!

The location of this photograph of July 1959 is the bottom of Box Hill, close by the lower end of St. Pancras Avenue. The cottage is Burrington Lodge, at that time the home of Leonard Shears. The road through the gate led to Burrington House.

Pathfields played an important role in rural life until the post-war housing estates obliterated many of them. The path in the foreground of this picture (note the stile) ran up the hill by Pennycross Barton, over the Devonport and Plymouth leats, down between the Beacon Park Rugby Ground and the old reservoir, and emerged into Beacon Park Road just opposite the well-known "Hole in the Wall".

Alan Davies of Pennycross recalls that the local lads used the hill in the foreground for tobogganning, usually finishing up in the Ham Brook.

(City Museum)

This picture is also of Honicknowle Lane in July 1959, just prior to the start of road widening.

The lane to the left originally led to Burrington House. This dated from the mid-17th century and was in the hands of the Were family until 1778. The House was partly rebuilt around 1825 and continued to be occupied until it was bombed in 1941 when, ironically, it was being used as the headquarters of the Bomb Disposal Squad.

Burrington Secondary Modern School was built on the site and opened in September 1958. Honicknowle Lane was already being widened at the beginning of 1960 when the City bought the Burrington Estate off the Trustee of the St. Aubyn Estates for some £40,000.

(City Museum)

You would be wrong if you thought that this picture of Crownhill was taken on a Sunday morning. In fact it was taken on a Wednesday in 1956. Admittedly it was January!

This was the scene at the crossroads looking south from Crownhill Fort. The main road from Forder Valley to St. Budeaux was at that time the A374. Behind the lorry can be seen Sydney Isbell's confectionery.

Crownhill Barracks dated from 1891 when the area to the right of the picture was just a parade ground. During the 1930s it was re-named in honour of Torquay-born Field Marshal Viscount Plumer (1857-1932) who had a distinquished military career lasting over more than fifty years.

In September 1939 Plumer was occupied by the 2nd Battalion, the East Yorkshire Regiment under Lt-Col. J. L. I. Hawksworth OBE. The commanding officer was Brigadier F. H. Witts DSO., MC. They went off to France as part of the 8th Infantry Brigade.

After the King's Shropshire Light Infantry moved to Seaton Barracks in 1965, Plumer was used to house troops displaced from the Royal Citadel while it was modernised.

(City Museum)

This view shows the corner of Tavistock Road with the B3373 to Tamerton Foliot.

The western side of Plumer Barracks was originally just the parade ground. The western boundary of the site was marked by the old Plymouth leat. In 1898 some married officers' quarters were erected and then in 1916 four red-bricked barrack blocks were added. The one in the picture faced Crownhill Fort.

Although the main road looks quiet enough in this photograph from April 1957, it was soon to become a "black spot" when the post-war motoring boom really gained momentum in the mid-1960s. The City had already made plans to ease the problem but were held up until 1965 when the Ministry of Defence finally agreed to swop Plumer Barracks for additional land around Seaton Barracks. This western side was to be vacated by January 1st 1966 and by September demolition was well under way, most of the debris being re-used at Manadon where a roundabout was under construction. The new road was opened in December 1967.

(City Museum)

This picture shows the western side of the Garrison Church of St. Alban. Its position can be placed by the "Danger Troops Crossing" sign in the photo on page 58.

Built at the same time as the barracks (1891/2), the final service was held here in September 1971. The organ was removed to Whitleigh Methodist Church.

The Reverend G. E. McNeill officiated in 1939. No permanent appointments were made during the War and afterwards St. Alban's was served from the Royal Citadel.

St. Alban's was photographed in January 1956.

(City Museum)

A tram route to Compton was first authorised in 1880 but the original company collapsed. It was bought out by Plymouth Corporation in 1892 and they constructed a horse tram line to Compton Lane End. A depot was built in Lower Compton Road and services started on April 3rd, 1893. Exactly eight years later the route was electrified.

The picture above was taken in January 1963 and shows the line which ran up an incline to the overhaul works. This had a traverser for moving trams from one line to another. The works was closed in 1928 when the main depot at Milehouse was finished. Compton Depot was last used to store spare trams for football specials.

In 1933 the depot was sold to the aptly named Plymouth Transport Company whose green and cream lorries used it until they were taken over in 1963 by Drake Carriers Ltd. Five years later they moved out. Flats, garages, a supermarket, a pub and even a block of offices were planned for the 2½ acre site but in 1973 a block of flats was erected to the designs of Marshman, Warren and Taylor.

(Brian Moseley)

In 1958 British Railways put into operation the first of a new breed of locomotive called Diesel-Hydraulics. With a weight of 117½ tons and a tractive effort of 50,000 lbs, they were lighter than a "Castle" class yet more powerful than a "King". Five were built by the North British Locomotive Company for the Western Region and all were used between Plymouth and Paddington. They were named after warships, *Active, Ark Royal, Bulldog, Conquest* and *Cossack*.

The first of these, Number D600 *Active*, made its first journey to Plymouth on Wednesday, March 19th, 1958. It hauled a ten coach special from Swindon and arrived a quarter of an hour earlier than expected after touching speeds of up to 90 mph. After refuelling, *Active* returned to Swindon.

On Monday, April 21st, 1958 *Active* was to have hauled the Cornish Riviera Express from Penzance to Plymouth but in the event a steam engine, 5049 *Earl of Plymouth*, brought the train up instead. D600 took an empty train to Penzance and back.

In fact the first run "in service" took place the following day and the photograph above shows the train after its arrival back at North Road Station.

(Western Morning News)

As mentioned on the previous page *Active* started revenue earning work on Tuesday, April 22nd, 1958. It left Plymouth at 4.50 a.m. with the previous night's 9.50 p.m. from Paddington.

Upon arrival at Penzance it had a couple of hours rest before taking on the prestigeous duty of being the first diesel to haul the Cornish Riviera Express, 10 a.m. off Penzance. After calling at St. Erth, Gwinear Road, Truro and Par, it then sped non-stop for just under an hour to arrive in Plymouth at around 12.20 p.m.

At 2.38 p.m. it left North Road again this time at the head of the down Cornish Riviera. The picture on this page shows it entering Saltash Station at just before a ten to three.

Active then returned from Penzance at 6.40 p.m. with the up mail train which after picking up mail bags from the lineside apparatus at Liskeard would have rushed through Keyham Station at 9 p.m.

In the above picture, note the apparatus for collecting the single line token in use on the Royal Albert Bridge. This system ceased in July 1961.

(Gilbert Corran)

When H.M.S. *Defiance* was launched at Pembroke Dock in 1861 she was the ninth to carry that name. Unfortunately she was built at a time when ironclads were just emerging so she was obsolete before she was completed. On December 13th, 1884 she became the torpedo training school ship at Devonport.

H.M.S. *Vulcan* was launched at Portsmouth on June 13th, 1889. Her armament comprised eight 4.7 inch guns and twelve 3 pounders. She was renamed *Defiance III* on February 17th, 1931 and became a depot ship for submarines. In June of that same year the original H.M.S. *Defiance* was sold for scrap and broken up in Millbay Docks.

The *Vulcan* continued to serve the Royal Navy although in 1934 there was talk of making it a shore base. These fears were renewed in 1948 when H.M.S. *Impregnable* was closed although in 1952 it was thought that H.M.S. *Devonshire* might be used instead.

However, on January 5th, 1954 it was announced that the School was "going ashore" and being moved to Portsmouth. The *Vulcan*, then 55 years old, is seen above being towed past Drake's Island in December 1955 on her way to a Belgian scrapyard.

(Western Morning News)